A Note to Parents and Teachers

DK READERS is a compelling reading programme for children, designed in conjunction with leading literacy e including Cliff Moon M.Ed., Honorary Fellow of the Uni of Reading. Cliff Moon has spent many years as a teacher teacher educator specializing in reading and has written 140 books for children and teachers. He reviews larly for teachers' journals.

Beautiful illustrations and superb full-colour photographs combine with engaging, easy-to-read stories to offer a fresh approach to each subject in the series. Each DK READER is guaranteed to capture a child's interest while developing his or her reading skills, general knowledge, and love of reading.

The five levels of DK READERS are aimed at different reading abilities, enabling you to choose the books that are exactly right for your child:

Pre vel 1 – Learning to read
Le   1   – Beginning to read
Le   2   – Beginning to read alone
Lev   3   – Reading alone
Level 4   – Proficient readers

The "normal" age at which a child begins to read can be anywhere from three to eight years old, so these levels are only a general guideline.

No matter which level you select, you can be sure that you are helping your child learn to read, then read to learn!

DK

LONDON, NEW YORK, MUNICH,
MELBOURNE AND DELHI

37

Series Editor Deborah Lock
Senior Art Editor Tory Gordon-Harris
Design Assistant Sadie Thomas
Production Claire Pearson
DTP Designer Almudena Díaz

Reading Consultant
Cliff Moon, M.Ed.

Published in Great Britain by Dorling Kindersley Limited
80, The Strand, London, WC2R 0RL
2 4 6 8 10 9 7 5 3 1

A Penguin Company

A CIP record for this book is available
from the British Library

ISBN 0-7513-1389-0

Colour reproduction by Colourscan, Singapore
Printed and bound in China by L Rex Printing Co., Ltd.

The publisher would like to thank the following for their
kind permission to reproduce their photographs:
a=above; c=centre; b=below; l=left; r=right t=top;

Corbis: David Cumming 18t; David Katzenstein 22c;
Michael Keller 30-31; **Food-Pix:** Susan Marie Anderson 26-27, 32bc.
Norman Hollands: 13bcr; **Stephen Oliver:** 12bc, 15bcr.

All other images © Dorling Kindersley.
For further imformation see: www.dkimages.com

see our complete catalogue at
www.dk.com

DK READERS

LEARNING
TO READ
pre-level **1**

Party Fun

DK

A Dorling Kindersley Book

How old are you?

invitation

crayons

Come to my

birthday party

On Saturday

At 3 p.m.

streamer

decorations

I had a
party yesterday.
I hung up the
decorations.

paper chain

I blew up the balloons and tied them up with string.

balloons

8

string

My friends came
in fancy dress.

hat

pig ear

My friends gave
me some presents.
What were they?

 presents

bow

I opened the
presents.
I had some
new toys.

car

toys

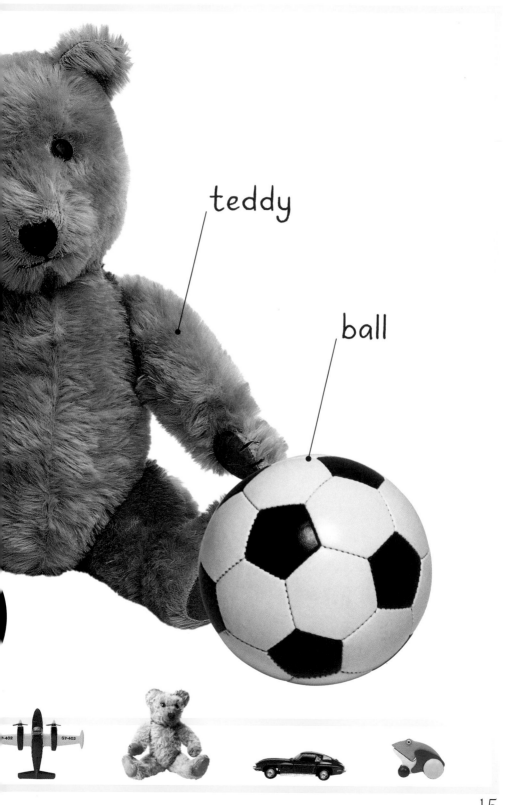

teddy

ball

red nose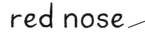

Then the
clown came.
He was very
funny.

clowns

finger puppet

puppets

The puppet show
was lots of fun.

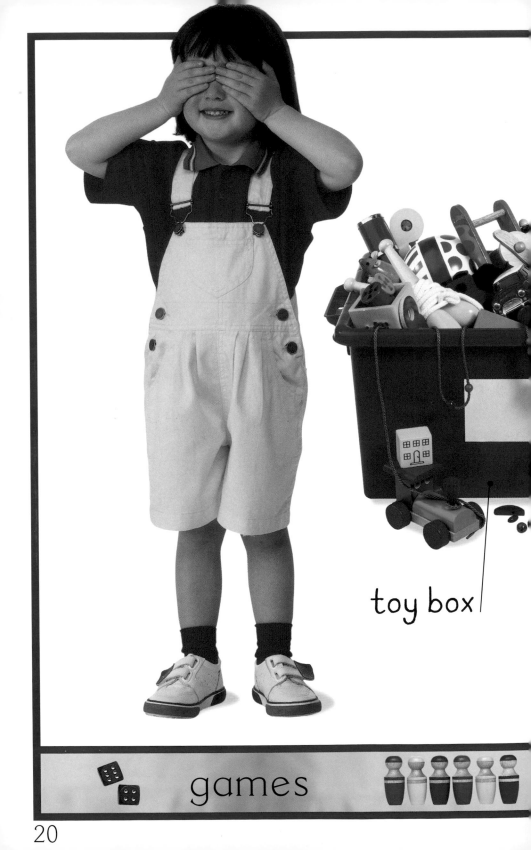

toy box

games

We played a
party game called
hide-and-seek.

hat

Then it was time
to eat the food.

ham

brea

food

cheese

I liked eating
the puddings
best.

strawberry

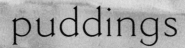

puddings

ice cream

nuts

I blew out the candles on my cake.

candle

 cakes

cake

treats

I gave my friends some party treats.

party hat

sweets

My friends said,
"Goodbye!"

When is your

birthday?

31

Picture word list

decoration
page 6

balloon
page 8

fancy dress
page 10

present
page 12

toy
page 14

clown
page 16

puppet
page 18

game
page 20

food
page 22

pudding
page 24

cake
page 26

treat
page 28